William Darwin Crabb

Silver Shimmer

William Darwin Crabb

Silver Shimmer

ISBN/EAN: 9783743320710

Manufactured in Europe, USA, Canada, Australia, Japa

Cover: Foto ©ninafisch / pixelio.de

Manufactured and distributed by brebook publishing software
(www.brebook.com)

William Darwin Crabb

Silver Shimmer

SILVER SHIMMER.

BY

WILLIAM DARWIN CRABB.

SAN FRANCISCO:

A. L. BANCROFT AND COMPANY,

Printers and Bookbinders.

1874.

THIS scant unequal Silver Shimmer
On the crystal sea
Of Poetry—
On whose deep sea these faint rhymes glimmer—
To her, the one who read them first,
Who most inspired them
And admired them;
Whose tropic heart hath interspersed
The sunshine of her sunny fate—
These glints of fancy, broken-versed,
These glints of song, I DEDICATE.

CONTENTS.

SILVER SHIMMER.

AN ASPIRATION.

I FEEL some deep and tall eternal aspiration
    tion
    For something out beyond the common
      whirl—
For music with a grander intonation
    Than even grand old Ocean's, in its swirl—
A lunging upward of the part immortal,
To catch a flying glimpse beyond "the portal !"

Last night mine eyes walked o'er the far embor-
    dered
    Blue heavens; and they strolled along its seas
Of silver clouds, and 'long the wild, unordered,
    Swift comet-rivers—leaned against its purple
      trees,

Whose buds are waving stars, whose tops do blossom
With suns and moons, which toss, O, far across
  them.

I thought I saw, trailed upward thro' the crimson
  Of sunset clouds, the shadow of that thought.
My soul leaps westward—leaps and swiftly swims
    on
  The crimson flood—I reach my hands, and it
    —is not !
My soul falls backward, sick from its exertion,
And feeling all desire amid its deep desertion.

This frets the flesh away—this trackless yearning—
  This pleading, everlasting call !
O this eternal reaching, and returning
  Heart-empty to this tame and barren ball !
Ah ! even Cleopatra's love were breastless,
When this aspiring adds *unrest* to *restless !*

THE GOLDEN GATE.

ERE stand two sun-lit battlements,
   The pillars of the Golden Gate.·
   They, many a year of olden date,
As angel-builded resting tents
   Have seemed to weary, beaten ships,
Which gleamed with eyes—with eyes untold
   That gazed above stern-bitten lips—
Dreamed dreams of Love, but gazed for gold.

A gate between of shining wave
   Swings out and in and everlasting.
Here feet find rest—some hearts, a grave,
   And hopes fulfill, or die of fasting.

And, as a mouth drilled thro' the mounts,
   It seems to breathe a breath of gold
   Out of the deep-gorged peaks that hold
Their mints of minerals and the founts
   Of blessed streams, with beds of treasure

And banks of wealth and blooming glory—
    Where Nature is eternal pleasure,
And trees are green, when Time is hoary.

And—like a large rich-laden flower
    Of gorgeous hue and deepest sweet
    Where bees crowd on with fretting feet—
The Bay blooms up, with under power,
    From ocean's heart of trembling blue ;
And men crowd on its restless rim,
    Where steeples tower and banners flow,
And sunny winds float sound of hymn.

The city of the Golden Gate—
    Shall she be built a grand and fit
    Metropolis? or she forget
The Builder of all good and great,
    Till He shall strike his fiery hand
Beneath the proud magnificent
    And sink her streets of hollow sand—
And sea-swirl lull her discontent?

Shall she become the dream fulfilled
    Of Poe's fantastic poetry—
    Become "The City in the Sea?"

And Ocean tread the iron-willed?
  And rocks rise up in wrath and close
The eye-entrancing Golden Gate,
  And leave it to a strange repose,
Or winds' and sea-waves' long debate?

A DOUBLE PROPHECY.

THE amethystine sky of youth is not
So brilliant purple, as it was of old.
I see much farther through the ways of
    men—
Can read, thro' human eyes, much deeper down
In hearts, the motives of the reckless world—
Can better make interpretation of
The touch of human hands, if they be true,
Or false—can see a buried, pallid sorrow
Hid 'neath the flowers and grasses of a laugh—
Can analyze a tear, if it be sweet
Or bitter—aye, am wiser in the ways
Of unaspiring earth.   But then I know
I cannot see so deep into sublime
Delightful skies.   The limit of my look—
My vision Heaven-ward, is drawing in.
No thought of God so pure, so high, so sweet,
But I could reach it with the finger tips
Of boyish faith, and touch the gems, and smile
With expectation of some better day

Wearing a crown beset with those sweet truths—
And then to promise better days was promise
Of loveliness indeed. The leaves seemed cut
In image of some truth, some bliss—seemed cut
With diamond of God's finger ; and the streams
Seemed pouring o'er the tongue of Nature to
God's sea of wisdom ; and upon those streams
I made my daily voyages, and drank
The boundless waters of this sea. The stars,
I held them in my hand, and praised their Maker.
There was no spirit tempest—no despair
Could sink them in the sea of sky—no doubt
Could stir its waves to toss them from my reach.
I held the hand of her of youthful beauty,
And followed in the trail of eye-gaze
That reached far nearer to the infinite
Than mine. 'Twas easy then to journey up
Unto the citadel of God. It seemed
The very angels wound their fingers round
Her ringlets, shimmering in the sun of health.
Her tread seemed ever bearing up ; and I
Reached up and after. The glory of the skies
Well had been proud of the resemblance of
Her mellow eyes—the glowing red of eve,
Been proud of kinship to the redness of
Her cheeks. The spirit, that did breathe the life

Into the universe, could press her soul,
It seemed to me, and not pollute it by
The touch.   'Twas in the May-time, and I had
Bethought myself insane to think THAT May
Of trust and joy would desolate, as Mays
Of seasons fall beneath the shrouds of winters.

My dreams were more delirious with delight
Even than the bubbling real.   But then the mind
Is half a prophet; and the things we spurn
As superstitions, by the reeling head
Of reason, retreat by day, and reattack
Us in the night, and pillage every citadel.
We waken in the morning, sad, at first,
Then call it superstition, and rebuild.
The capture of a joy, the stabbing of
A hope, the murder of a love are all
Preacted in our dreams; and yet we laugh
And call it superstition.   *So with me:*
When flowers were at their fullest, and the grass
Was colored emerald, and when the moon
Bloomed brightest of the May, then stars began
To tremble (in my dream) along the west
And toss beyond my reach—then one by one
Sink in the rolling of a distant storm.
The moon began to shake upon its stem,

And then it laid its face beneath the flood,
Which still came nearer. Now the roof sounded
    with the roar
Of winds and waters. Flowers broke from their
    stems
And rolled in the mud, and then were sunken
In water, as the stars had sunk. I could
Not see far up, and, as I gazed about
Upon the washing, wasting earth, I thought
Of *her* ; and she was distant ; and the waves
Had tossed between us; and the drift of wrecks
Too thick to number, struggled out in ruin.
The waves grew thick with muddiness at times,
Then rushed with fury on; and waifs and wood,
In pieces, piled around my feet. I cried!
But seething of the waves and battering
Of floating pieces outspoke my utterance:
And then I looked and saw she, whom I loved,
Was drowning in the sea—drifting beyond
The reach of me forever. This was a dream.
I wakened with the superstition deep
Upon my soul ; and then I combed the tangles
Out of my locks, and combed the superstition
Out of my brain with the electric teeth
Of thoughtless laugh ; then ran to meet my —
    nameless.

But she had wed another, strange and tall !
An avalanche of snows had slidden down
Upon me in one night ; and all the glow
And glory of the mountain foot and vale
Had shrivelled in a night.   I cast my looks
Up to the former amethystine skies—
They hung a broad and ebon coffin lid,
Too mighty for my feeble strength to lift,
Too hard to penetrate, to get above,
And so I could but turn to digging down,
And sinking deeper in the treacheries
And lower wisdom of this barren world.

Leaves now seem handkerchiefs of Nature, hung
Shaking before my face in mockery;
And I have wandered from those streams that
      flow
Into God's sea; and dust from fruitless digging
Of grumbling men worries me on—and yet
Sometimes I would aspire again.   The thoughts
Of that luxuriant summer I have seen
Come, in my musing, and convert the frail
And flickering spirit fire, I kindled as
My sun went down, into the image of
A balmy May sun ; and my chamber walls
Of marble color turn to amethyst ;

And stars hang in the window, and I reach
To handle them—and then I start, and mutter:
" 'Tis but a superstition!"   But the *heart*
Says this is real.   So I've come to call
Our dreams and reveries the deepest truth—
The prophets of our active lives.   Here is
The remnant of my hope, *that this day-revery*
Doth prophesy the restoration of
What vanished with fulfillment of a dream.

2

TALES OF A BORDER TAVERN.

IT. was a place where people mix
    Of all grades up from the border "bricks"
    And men of the gentler, polished tricks,
  To men of morals and minds correct
As Pharisees after the strictest sect.
It was a place of diet rough,
Of diet scarce, but jokes enough.
It was a place of creviced faces
And hanging heads and troubled paces.
It was a place where many a man
Has held his head in a cloud of smoke,
Seated aside, as if a ban
Had driven him out o' the midst o' folk.
It was a place where many a one
Has sat and smoked and stories spun
And watched the smoke curl up and off,
His mind, on the wings of every puff,
Flowing away to another time—
To an olden love in another clime.
It was a night in January;

And a "norther" had just swept down
Driving the sunny day from town,
" Swift and cold as the very scratch,"
As the landlord said.   " Thunder ! very!"
Said the lawyer, lighting a tuft of grass
To light his pipe instead of a match,
At the same time grasping the wooden latch
And slamming the door till it shook the glass.
The place was hard and the people, too;
And yet as I write is written true;
A rough truth's better'n smooth-tongued lies.
The cold north wind had whipped us in,
And the bar was full of smoke and men,
And ruffian thoughts and plots of sin,
That warred the silent memories
Coaxing us back to calmer seas,
Coaxing us out o' the horrid din
Back to memories sweet as youth—
Back to memories strong as truth !
" Hello ! Rick Dane, ye old consarn !
Ef you ain't here !   Now spin us a yarn—
Best in the market.   Come! none o' yer slang,
But spit out yer yarn !" shouted a man
With a look of rock—yet, nine to ten,
His heart was flesh.   "Well, let me hang,"
Muttered Rick Dane, " Ef you come to find

This chap in duty, or yarns behind !"
The dreamy eyes of a lazy boast
Suddenly rose from their bed o' sleep,
As he saw Dane's face grow sad as a ghost,
And he said to us: "I look fur a heap
O' stirrin' story fro' Rick to-night;
Fur his face is ez long ez the 'moral law;'
An' suthin' has given his brave heart fright—
There's suthin' a troublin' his mental craw!"
"Well, then, if I must, I must, I 'spose;
So fill me a pipe—there ! Boys, here goes!
But, 'fore I begin, let the laziest man
Stir up the fire—en' thet's you, Dan!
Hurrah! for a thrust at the red-hot blaze!
Ho! for whiff on whiff, till a blue smoke-maze
Shall be unto me and the yarn I tell
As a lady's veil, in throwin' a spell
O' increased beauty over the veiled!
Yes, ho! fur a thrust in the deep red fire,
And a deeper thrust in a redder heart!
Blaze up, old fire, you're rude assailed!
Go up, old bald head smoke—aspire,
Ez the Scripturs say! Now I'm ready to start."

RICK DANE'S STORY.

I've rid on these borders when
I tell ye 'twaz awfully rough

With winds and the dust and thousands
 Uv other sich horrible stuff.
Ez the preacher would hev it—but give me
 A whiff to open the way!
Whew! somebody stir up the fire;
 Fur the very devil's to pay
I should say from the speed o' the wind!
 And, boys, the cut uv its whizz
Reminds me o' many a blusterin'
 Night with a rushing o' biz
Thet wuz bloody ez butchers!—but somehow
 Or 'nother I haven't the nack
O' keepin' the text, so I've gotten
 A good ways out o' the track.
Well, the time I am speakin' uv, boys,
 It wuz a night thet wuz dark
Ez the landlord's hands, sometimes,
 When he stirs the fire fur a spark
With the other end o' the poker—
 A night ez wuz still ez if stark,
Ez tho' thet the air wuz a lump
 Ez hard and ez black ez a coal.
It wuz a time, boys, ez when thet
 The price uv a human soul
Wuz ez cheap ez the price uv a " lager,"

An' sometimes scurcely ez dear—
When the towns wuz ez scattered an' few .
    Ez eyes that never a tear
Hez ever run out uv—besides, boys,
    The few little towns thet thur waz
Wuz treacherous places, you bet,
    And laughed at the nonsense o' " laws."
Well, I wuz a-lodgin', one night,
    In one o' them treacherous places;
I hed been on a hunt that day,   .
    And hed jest got out o' the traces
An' turned into bed, to think
    Uv the times when I wuz a boy,
An' think uv a hand ez wuz wrinkled
    And old and trembly, an' toy
With a hand ez wuz young an' steady
    And smooth as the ball o' yer eye,
An' chuck at a chin ez—but that is
    A matter o' her an' I!
I'm tellin' o' when I wuz lodgin'
    In one o' them treacherous towns.
Ez hard as a flint, it wuz,
    Comparin' its morals to stones.
I lay on my bed for a minit—
    Then suthin' disturbed me, ez if

The voice o' distress, or the like
    Hed given my spirit a "diph."
I turned, an' I listened, but then
    Thar wuzn't the sign uv a sound—
An' I know'd it was only a kind
    Uv a fancy a flittin' around.
But still, ez I lay on my bed,
    Thar wuz suthin' kept tellin' to me:
"Go down to the street that is under
    The hill, Rick Dane, an' see !"
I laughed at myself fur bein'
    A suddent a tremblin' slave
To only a kind uv a fancy,
    That boasted myself so brave.
And yet ez I laughed there wuz suthin'
    That kept up a pitiful callin':
"Go down to the street, an' go
    The house, uv the lime-stone wall, in—
To the street down under the hill,
    An' rescue a star that is fallin'!"
A man that is ever so brave,
    To a danger that's said in the ear,
When it's said to the sperit, may set him
    A feelin' almighty queer.
I laughed as a crazy man does,

Wi' not very much o' the feelin'
Uv laughter into my soul ;
   Fur I feared some feller was " heelin' "
Some one ez wuz better'n', worthier'n',
   The rest uv us rowdies that roved—
Some one ez wuz better 'un us,
   An' God an' the angels loved ;
An' which they had whispered to me:
   "Ef I would go down to the street—
Step into the shoes uv one
   That hed purer and youthfuller feet,
And, if need be, die fur the same!"—
   Well, I finally riz
And went to the door a minit,
   To listen ef there wuz the whizz
Uv bullets in hearin' ; if so
   To go to the place o' the " biz."
Then I went to the wall that wuz lime-stone
   On the street that wuz under the hill.
I stood—and, exceptin' the chug
   Uv my breast, it wuz terrible still—
When, shortly, an' all uv a suddent,
   The scream uv a woman burst
Out o' that house infernal,
   Wi' voices o' men accurst !

I broke in the door in a rush ;.
  And, back in the horrible room,
Three cowardly cut-throat men,
  More devilish thar in the gloom,
Threatened, with knife and pistol,
  A woman that jest hed begin
  To drop the blossom o' purity
  Under the frost o' sin.
'Twuz only a minit—and thar's whar
  I got this scar—d'ye see?
And them three men went—well—whar
  God is judge, not me!
I felt it wuz perfectly right, fur
  Suthin' within kept callin':
"This is the liftin' o' her that
  Only a little is fallen!"
She said "For the sake of a love . . . . !
  But I'm going to cleanse this breast ;
For, because I have lost a part,
  Then why should I lose the rest?
When God has made me as pure
  As I was when I was a girl,
I'll write to you, the angel
  That saved me, and send you a curl."
So why should I be too hard
  On a woman ez only wuz wild

To run away fro' the thoughts
  O' the times when she wuz a child,
When I wuz doin' the same ?
  We forgive the folly o' men;
Then why not her, who went back to the
    right,
  While men go on in their sin ?—
Hure is the yeller curl
  An' these are the words she wrote:
" I've kept my word, and God
  And the angels have helped me out.
If now I am not so pure as
  When I was a girl, I know
That, ere this letter you read,
  I'll be purer—be whiter than snow.
For shadows of earth are going
  Down, and a beautiful light
Is showing my spirit up !
  God bless you! you started me right!"
So, boys, be still, fur her spirit
  Is near, an' thet is enough
To smooth the waves o' my heart
  Thet usually run so rough !

Rick Dane was done; and a silent spell
Over the group a moment fell.

Then an old man, up to his eightieth year,
Turned sharp on me, and said—"Look here!"

THE OLD MAN'S STORY.

UP THE MISSOURI.

You're one o' them fellers the world has give
    The tipsy name uv a " genis "—
Whose eyes look up 'neath the skirts o' the skies,
    Ez the blossoms and leaves which green is.
You're one o' them fellers as never has lifted
    A hand or taken a stroke in
The world of work; but only has written
    O' hearts ez are splintered and broken.
You're one o' the few ez God has made
    Fur suthin' ez turned to a dreamer—
Thet God has given the glory 'f a flag
    Ez turned to only a streamer—
Thet the clamorin' herd, ez the poets say,
    Has crowned your head wi' laurels;
Yet never has fought a lick, but writ
    O' the unpoetical quarrels—
With heart ez a girl's, an touched, ez easy
    Ez to fall from a tree, with pity;
Too poor to give to the sufferer anything more
    Than a most uneatable ditty—

One o' them fellers ez in your songs
    Uproots the biggest o' mountains,
But then, ez to facts, don't lift the tiniest pebbles
    Thet shines at the edge o' the fountains—
One o' them rambling fellers, I 'spose,
    Thet hez some sort uv a mission
That's out o' the reach o' the computation
    O' "simple addition."

This world is real enough—too real for many a
      one,
    Who started with good decision.
Perhaps you fellers are here to fool us, at times,
    With a fanciful touch Elysian.
You're one o' them fellers ez rambles around
    And gathers a line from each human,
From "the man in the ditch" and the only
    Charity-shunned of earth, a woman
Low in the dust o' sin, to the man thet glitters
    In gold and the jewels taken
From this same woman, on whom he has rolled
    The rock of a curse and crushed her and left
      her forsaken.
You're one o' them fellers ez wanders around after
    A line on love an' a salable story—

To turn the grief uv a brother, deep ez a heart,
    to a song
To lengthen your tower uv glory!

Now, I am a man of little to say; the devil I care
    For the pettier woes thet worry
The greedier world; but my word's ez sure
    Ez the sun, tho' I talk in a hurry.
I hev no lies of love—no flashin' words
    To build a palace o' fiction;
But I hev the logs o' facts to build a cabin o' truth,
    To tell in a humble diction.
So shake your girlish tresses off o' yer face,
    And I will open this locket !
And tell me now ef a worthier eye
    Rolls in a human socket ?
Or yit of the universe-eye, the blue sky, is—
    Tossed in its place, whose tears are started
By the love o' God pervadin' creation, an' even
    The heart o' the broken-hearted ?
On that side is *her*, on this is the child, jest the
    pictur
O' her, wi' face to the face o' the mother;
An' that is the way their faces stood that time
    on the bank,
    One face and heart to the other.

You may laugh at the thought, your hair's the same
 Ez the hair of that three year girl's ;
But then if yer heart's az pure an' ez wise as her's,
 Ye needn't be 'shamed o' yer curls.
Well, how them two are gone from me now,
 And their faces are set in a locket—
How two sweet souls went up, ez a bird, and my
  sperits down
 Ez the dyin' blaze uv of a rocket,
Is this: 'Twas only a step to the bank, an' the
  snows
 Had started a terrible freshet,
For this wuz the time, speakin' ez men o' cattle,
 The meltin' snows o' the mountains "flesh it."
And her, whose hair wuz like ez to yourn, went
  down to   .
 The edge, and set to a lookin' under
And thinkin' them dreamy things, ez you poets!
 I see now thet was a blunder
To let her go thar; her ma saw then, and called;
 But her call wuz lost in the thunder
Uv muddy Missouri !—she shot
 Like the flash uv an eye, and under
Her arms she gathered the child ; and, jest as
 she turned
 So I see the glow o' their faces,

And our hearts clumb up to the highest limb, an'
    a shout
    O' rejoicin' mixed in wi' the roar o' the masses,
The water-beast butted his turbulent horns
    Mad into the bank—so my darlings
Went down wi' the sand, an out uv my reach,
    With a cry, ez the cry uv the starling's—
(It's a story the mother related my child of a
    starling
    Ez cried with a tremble o' pity,
" I can't get out !" an' this is the cause o' my
    figur.
    It happened somewhar in a city.)

So you see why I tuk my locket and went fro,
    home ;
    For how cud I stay in a dwellin'
Where tongues o' fire and cloven wuz set on all
    That I see, a burnin' an' tellin'
O' what wuz no more—an' tellin' o' slidin' banks,
    Jest down beside o' the thicket,
Where, 'stead o' the voices o' two, is only the
    single
    Trill uv a hermit cricket !

    One long breath and a single glance
From each o' the curious audience ;

Then a little silence—a sad suspense,
  When the lawyer suddenly broke the trance: ..

THE OLD LAWYER'S STORY.

Them times, when I wuz a young man,
  Warn't ez times is now.
We studied our law from nature,
  And only studied ez how
This un was guilty, or that un,
  And not how to pick out a flaw
With technical words, or suthin',
  And spile the justice o' law.
Thar wuzn't no need uv a scholar,
  Or a head crammed full o' the books
Thet lawyers of cities were usin',
  But jest to know uv the crooks
Thet ort to be straightened, to show
- The ekety into the case—
And the best way o' knowin' wi' us wuz
  To look at the criminal's face.
Them wuz the times when ruffins
  Done the most o' the " biz."
An' all the lawyers I knowed uv
  Waz them ez pled wi' the whizz
O' bullets an' sich, an' so
  I warn't but little use—

O' course I done my levelest
  To gabble agin abuse.
But then I used my judgment
  Of when, an' how, an' whar,
And didn't risk my life
  On a pint o' law too far.
Ef ever a place on arth
  Could hev a 'proprit name,
That could hev " necessity,"
  Which an' it wuz the same ;
Fur it knowed no law, exceptin'
  The little I knowed—you bet
I knowed I better keep low—
  I wuz lawyer enough fur that. . . . .

In the little town—no matter
  What the name o' the place is—
The streets was full uv a sea
  Uv rough up-lookin' faces ;
An', (in the middle o' all this
  Tide o' tanny grins,
An' eyes ez deep as wells
  An' dim wi' the dust o' sins;
An' beards ez grizzled ez law books,
  Tossed up wi' the sea, and down
Over the lawless bosoms

An' under the foams o' frown)
Thar ther wuz *one* face 'o beauty,
   Like a drop o' melted gold
Afloat in a sea o' brass.
   Then I wuzn't quite so old;
An' it set me hard a-thinkin',
   What in the course o' life
Hez throwed this orange o' beauty
   Into the mire?   What knife
Haz stolen into the garden
   And cut her off o' the tree
And throwed her over the walls
   Into this muddy sea?"
I wuz younger then than now,
   I would hev the court to know,
An' I wuz a jedge o' beauty,
   Ez well ez a jedge o' law—
I'z a jedge o' human natur,
   I beg yer leave to say,
An' I saw in a minit, thet, though
   Her heart hed a tetch o' *gray*,
I could make it plain to a jury
   Thet it wazn't *black* wi' sin—
Thet thar wuz a question of whether
   The devil or God would win.
Thinks I, in a minit more,

Ef Christ forgiv the thief
And pardoned the fallen woman,
  I'm right in my belief,
There's a chance o' savin' her.
  So I wedged through the surly crowd,
Till I teched the scarlet woman—
  An' my heart it beat aloud,
For fear I 'uz makin' a blunder;
  But I spoke in a kindly way;
An' ez quick ez the snap uv a trigger
  She turned; an' a' little spray
O' blushes flew up her face,
  An' a glance o' mystery
Come out o' the fine red ground work
  Thro' the jewel uv her eye.
I mentioned about a sister
  Ez purty ez even her,
And how 'twould 'a' broke my heart
  To see her whar she were;
An' I tol' uv another girl
  She set me a-thinkin' uv—
An' how 'twould 'a' driv me mad
  To 'a' seen her a soiled dove.
Fur a minit the glance in her eye,
  Ez a shiny piece o' gold,
Dropped back in her rily soul—

An then come out more bold!
Then, ez we walked away,
    She lowered her head a bit,
An' I saw her brow grow set,
    And her bosom lift, an' a grit
Uv her teeth, ez went like a chill
    Over my mind; and she said:
" Over the eastern hills—
    A pity that I'm not dead !—
And up in the little school
    On the side o' the olden hill,
I stood at the head o' my class,
    And my little ship on the rill
Was first o' the little fleet. . . . .
    Time bore me away to school,
Out o' the love o' home,
    And into the chill o' rule:
And all o' the lore o' books,
    And all o' the polished ways
That money could buy were mine.
    But, oh! in the flow of days
And out o' the love o' home,
    And out o' the love of all,
I caught at the eye of a passing one,
    And his voice began to call.
A love sprang up in my desert,

And stolen interviews;
And so, as my love 'gan gaining,
    My fears began to lose.
Ah! I was too young to know
    That so much belonged to me,
And to know that a thief would trouble—
    "Well, *here I am*—you see !"

And so we parted.   I watched
    To see whar the woman went,
Fur the roughened veil that covered
    My sympathies wuz rent.
And soon, ez I passed the street,
    In a thoughtful sort o' streak,
I saw her look out uv a window,
    And a tear crep' down her cheek.
Thet night, ez the moon come up,
    I stole from the noisy bar
To the shade uv a vacant dwellin',
    Thet slept beneath a star—
Leaned thar in sight o' the window,
    Thet her tear hed glistened through;
An' the sky waz over-speckled
    With stars, an' over blue.
An' the moon shone in her window,
    The only light wuz thar,

Exceptin' Mars uv a blood-red,
   Ez tho' 'twuz a symbol star
Shining into her room,
   Ez a symbol uv her wo.
The other stars wuz so lofty
   And her life wuz down so low
Thet they couldn't reach the woman;
   An' so, ez I sed, red Mars
Wuz glimmerin' thro' the glasses,
   And that wuz all uv her stars.
Then a broken-hearted voice
   Come out on the air to me:
" God, give me a broken spirit !
   God give me the will o' Thee ! "
The red-lit Mars, ez an eye
   Weepin' tears o' blood, gleamed
Silently over her fingers,
   And the moon above 'em beamed
Whiter than if foretelling
   Uv marble above her head.
I heard her pray repentance
   Fur " a pity that I'm not dead ! "
Her head bowed in the shadow,
   And then, as a ghost uv love,
It rose in the marbly moonlight,
   Ez her hopes went down or above—

Rose on the marbly moonlight,
  Jest ez her spirit fought
The dark way o' livin' she oughtn't,
  Then the light way o' livin' she ought.
Then again the broken voice
  Come out on the air to me:
"God, give me a broken spirit!
  God, give me the will o' Thee!
But, Jesus, thou knowest the stain
  That covers the all I am;
And the world will not forget it,
  Though my soul grow sweet as balm.
Thou knowest the pure in spirit,
  But the world is not so wise—
To the wayward their words are mercy
  Not till the wayward dies!
And, oh! could the will o' Thee
  Have it that I should go
Out o' the world o' hisses,
  Let it be so! for, oh!
Mine is so wayward a heart
  It wanders away from Thee!"

Then it seemed to me, as I listened,
  There was suthin' that I could see
Like a fluttering spirit flash   ..

Out thro' the window light,
And then, like a fleeing comet,
　Go off in the silent night.
Mebbe 'twuz only a fancy,
　Or the flash o' my falling tear,
But I b'lieve 'twaz the soul o' the woman
　Leaving her fallen sphere;
For she never went out o' her room,
　And she never arose from her kneeling,
Till we lifted her into a coffin,
　While rough eyes filled with feeling.

The ranchman rose, and began to pace,
As a thought danced over his grizzled face,
And said, with much more force than grace:

THE RANCHER'S STORY.

Wall, an' I'll say my say, fur the reason why
　That it is my turn, it is, an' I
Must say mine afore ol' Haller 'ill tell—
　And thet is the reason fur why,
An' not ez that I am any yer swell,
A takin' a sorryful tale-tellin' spell.

Wall, to be short, then, it wuz a ranch;
   An' ranches they warent ez thick
Them times ez now they be.   'Twas down on a
   branch
O' the Brazos—you've been on the very spot,
   Rick—
And the rancher he waren't so wealthy ez I—
The one I'm a speakin' uv—this uz the reason
   fur why:

He wuz suthin' o' polish, or suthin'
   Uv sich like a word that book-men say, ez I've
   heerd.
There waren't no book, or no language — no
   nuthin'
   That he didn't know uv; so ez thet he appeared
   Ez sharp as the lightnin', an' double geared.
They sed that he " broke" in a queer kind o' way,
Once back in the east, an' atween a night an' a
   day,
Hed to start up, wi' a patterin' heart, an' fly—
So he's poorer 'an me, thet's the reason fur why.

One thing thet be sure, thar wuz, ez I'd vote,
   The ungodliest queer-like tossin' an start
Uv his rascalish eye ; an' I'd put up my coat,
   Thar wuz suthin' stept heavy inside on his heart

In the tenderest places—but thet's neither you
    nor I!
Fur it's out o' the subjic', an' thet's the reason
    fur why.

He wuz poorer, an' yet he wuz richer ez me;
    Leastwise none o' us ranchers cud buy the
        chap out.
For he had one lump o' treasure, you see,—
    A treasure, you see, ez would put to the rout
Yer millions uv gold an' ranches; and thet
Wuz a bright little girl; an', you bet,
Thar warent no thing—'cept God—cud get
Thet gay leetle blossom, an' thar warn't no use
    fur to try—
An' so he wuz richer ez me; *thet's* the reason
    fur why.

God kept her a-livin' a time, ez mebbe he might
    Meller the hard man's heart, perhaps.
    But God wuzn't going to let her to stay
    Till she grew so old ez to hev the same hard
    way.
So, when the years begin to grow to thet pint, a
    blight
    Gets up an' out o' the Brazos, an' taps

Et the rancher's door; an' the darlin' she let's it
    in.
  So it eats et this jew'l o' this man o' sin
  Till she grows ez slim an' thin-limbed ez a
    pin—
Till she bended down, ez a withery blossom stem,
An' her face dipped down i' the dust o' the earth,
  Ez the flower on the tip o' thet stem, the same!
So thar another burden o' dirt wuz throwed on
    his box o' mirth.

Then he dirted his knees wi' the dust thet wuz
    coverin' her;
  An' he used to say: "O the clouds hang low!
And my life's as a wall, and the clouds be big wi'
    myrrh,
  And they break on my life, as a wall; and so
They run so low they keep a breaking, and oh!
    Baptizing it over wi' myrrh as bitter as woe!"

Then he stole her up, an' gathered her up an'
    burned
His jew'l to ashes—they say—an' urned
The same! Then, ez a ghost, he vanished away.
Now, I reckon he's somwhar bearin' his urn to-
    day!—

With thet strange kind uv a-tossin' about uv his
    eye,
Which no one knows the terrible reason fur why.

———

A tale is but breath,
    Yet life is a tale
Borne over, by Death,
    And told in a wail,
Or in sweetness, hereafter.

Our lives are but tales
    Told in accents of pathos
Of loves under veils—
    Told in burnings of passion,
In tempests of wails,
    In flashes of wit,
In songs, in curses—
    In all, every whit,
Lives are tales!

PILGRIM'S PROGRESS.

[Being the biography of a *modern* pilgrim in verse.]

CANTO ONE.

LOW down upon the Mississippi river,
  Where balminess was king the most o'
    year,
Where's more of heat and more of languid fever
  Than chilly days and tingling toe and ear,
Where's less of bleeding lungs than bile upon the
    liver—
  Here, in a little town—its name shall not ap-
    pear—
There dwelt a lowly family of two,
Wherein, one morning, there was some ado.

One morning in the balmy month of June,
  (I said before it was not balmy all the year),
'There was a bustle in the little town;
  And matrons to and fro began to steer,
And, meeting at the corners, whisper undertone
  A secret each into another's ear—

But whisper confidentially, of course—
What was it? marriage, cradle, or a hearse?

The saucy boys quit kicking up their heels,
    Each hangs about the corner for a chance
To steal behind some matron, as she deals
    This secret to a friend, with cautious glance—
Forgets to cry for toys, forgets his meals,
    Hands punched into the pockets of his pants—
Forgets *all*, but his big desire to hear
The news that's setting all the town on ear.

The fact is this—to keep the ball in motion
    That set the town in such a fermentation,
And proved so bring-the-dead-to-life a potion—
    The fact is this—confuse my trepidation,
I scarce can say it! may be its a notion,
    But then a child new-born into temptation
I hate to think, or speak of.   But the fact
Is Pilgrim's born, *was* born, to be exact.

Hence those mysterious, knowing words and
        winks
    Of sly-tongued advocates of generation;
And clamorous boys with their "by Georges" and
        "by Jinks"—
    One gossip finally told all creation,

So I, at length, got hold one of the links
And dragged up all the chain—hence this inva-
sion
Of household rights—in other words, this story;
For which I'm paid in criticism, not glory.

O, for the innocence of heart I knew,
When, standing by my mother's side, I gazed
On Pilgrim, wondering at the great ado
Over so small a thing, and stood amazed
At all they said of good and beautiful and true
And great accomplishments that would be
blazed
Around the world connected with his name!
Ah! surely, thought I, he is born to fame!

That's nothing new or rare; for scores or more
Are born to fame in every rushing year,
But bred, alas! upon another score—
Born in the tumult of expectant cheer,
But bred to disappointment—to deplore
Their loss of innocence and all that's dear.
Biographies begin with "born—and bred,"
As though beyond some things remained unsaid

Of great importance—something grand, sublime,
Before we write the final sentence—*Dead!*

'Twould save a deal of trouble and of time
  To start with *born and dead*, instead
Of *born and bred*; for life is like a rhyme,
  Over a very great expanse is spread,
Yet might be written in a single line—
The same thing o'er and o'er like a repine.

Well, then, to hasten on the hero, I
  Will pass by twelve or sixteen years or so;
For babies only eat, and laugh, and cry,
  And boys are saucy, all alike, you know;
Hence, as I said, I pass those two times by,
  And introduce the hero proper—So
I take him up again, as in the verses
  That follow this, wherein I speak of hearses.

God! do I hear, then, yonder damned bell
  Pour groans for dead from out its brazen lips?
Accursed crown! I reel beneath thy knell,
  Which strikes my heart down like a sledge,
      and rips
A half-well wound! No sound resounds so fell
  As bell-knolls; for their tolling never drips
Upon my mind like music, since the time—
No matter—that was in another clime!

I see a box of varnished ebony,
  Lined with fine silk and velvet, white as purity—

With glinting silver studs ; and hinged, I see,
  With gleamy gold. How fair! Yet not se-
    curity
Against the pain of the bereft, who cry
  Around the dead ; nor yet against the ob-
    scurity
That waits the *favored* sleeper; for to sleep
The sleep is better than to live to weep,

And follow out the one within the coffin.
  But let me tell you who it is that's dead,
For fear you think it's Pilgrim—still more often
  The world would not be bothering its head ,
About who died, but turn and go to laughin'
  Before the hearse has wheeled a rod, instead
Of asking, with a sad face and a serious,
Who now has gone to try the dread mysterious?

A person's thoughts at best are like wild cattle;
  They always come in droves and out of order—
Not like a well-drilled army going to battle,
  More like the bison on the Kansan border.
So we must catch them while we can. What
    rattle
They make stampeding on the fertile plain
Within a bold and mighty genius' brain !

4

Because of this unsteady rushing in
  Of incoherent droves of thought, you see,
I wander from the straightest, strictest line
  Of this biography.   But let me be
Permitted here to say, as said before herein,
  Pilgrim "grew up," as people say.   To agree
Was not his father's and the Pilgrim's mode of
      action—
His mother, though, prevented serious faction.

It was not Pilgrim who was dead ; but, what
  Is worse, it was his mother.   Even those
Who think the very most of life would not
  Dissent from this opinion far, God knows.
She was a noble mother, all folks thought—
  As for his father, judging from his nose,
He was not quite so noble; so, you see,
Poor Pilgrim's show—but I must go to tea!

      .   .   .   .

Well, I have been to tea, and drunk it too,
  Although I think it isn't healthy very;
And coffee hurts the nerves, I always knew,
  Yet, like a toper, save not quite so merry,
I always drink them both, and so do you.
  I know I'd better be a toper cheery
Than growling with dyspeptic melancholy
  Brought on by swilling tea and coffee, Ollie!

I beg your pardon, I did not intend
  The world should know that you are standing
      here,
And that your kisses, on my forehead, send
  A rush of inspiration through—no matter where,
But I suppose the heart, tho' some would say the
      mind.
  Fair Ollie, now I promise, yea I swear
I'll never use your name again in verse;
So kiss my lips forgiveness—here's my purse!

Go, then, and purchase anything you please—
  (Cash keeps the most of women out of pets.
It will, if anything on earth, appease
  A displeased woman. Strange that man for-
      gets (?)
This fact so often. Though she is a tease,
  She's sweet. Who bets by her wins all his
      bets.)
Sweet Ol—but then I swore that, in my verse,
I'd name thee not, for better or for worse.

So goes it; few perhaps are happier, brighter
  Than when first wed—But what has that to do
With Pilgrim? (or with me? you ask. Ah! I'm
      a writer;
  And authors' private lives are *theirs*, you know.)

Poor Pilgrim's show, (I started out to cite, or
    I rather 'gan to write, sometime ago,
When I was called to tea,) was rather slim
For happy home.   His eyes were all a-swim

With great big tears; and many genuine snuffles
    Were smothered in his handkerchief, the while
A hand, as thoughtless as the shovel, shuffles
    The heavy, thumping clay down, with a will,
Upon the stupid dead.   Ah ! how it ruffles
    The Tahoe of his heart, so crystal still!
And how it roils the clear, with every clod
That falls upon his heart and dead, O God!

'Tis sad to see the last leaves fall and float
    Off on the chilly stream to some broad bay
To mingle with the drift of many a boat,
    Shattered and tossing helpless night and day
Upon its top-pitched swell; 'tis sad to note
    The fade of twilight; it is sad to lay
The last sunbeam upon the couch of night
And know that, ere it wakes, some soul takes
        flight;

'Tis sad to see the last brown, deadened blade
    Of grass buried beneath the first white snow
Of winter; 'tis sad to hear, across the glade,

The mellow song of some lone bird, and know
That, when its plaintive, dying notes shall fade
  To silence, 'tis the last; 'tis sadder, though,
'To follow out the best friend—as a wave,
A body, dead, afloat—to a silent grave !

His was a massive mind; and it was proud.
  Ill could he brook the horrid incubus
Of drunken tyranny. He had not bowed,
  Before his mother's death, to a "drunken cuss,"
And would not now! Hard words, yet thus he
    vowed.
  Oh ! "by the dogs !" how I despise a muss!
So I will pass it by, and give the issue:
He ran away!! Poor Pilgrim, Heaven bless
    you !

Come kiss me, O sweet, Ol——(no, spare her
    name!)
  By this I mean I want new inspiration:
For now I sing of love. 'Tis luck for fame
  That he was thrust, by such "concatenation
Of fortuitous circumstances," where he came
  To meet fair Lilie. O sweet expectation,
Buzz, as a humming bird, about and utter
Your honeyed promises and smile and flutter!

Oh! she was loveliness itself, fair Lilie, *
  And purer than a white-lipped lily's flower,
And not, like most of girls at sixteen, silly.
  Her great eyes beggar all descriptive power.
And they had looked on timid Pilgrim, till he
  Seemed floating on their violet tide. No hour
Was long, when she was with him; when away
A minute seemed a lonesome, lingering day.

But it would take a most stupendous volume
  To write up all the course of this true love—
How it did blind their prudence, how enthrall
    them.
  I'll not say what a futile fancy wove
Around them; or say what a flashing column
  Of crumbling sweets, a-gilt with fickle love,
They built by moonlight—and they never thought
That what seems "is" turns out more oft "is
    not."

I'll not here say how, when they ventur'd near
  Each other, (as two little crystal lakes,
The size of silver dollars, do appear
  To rush together for each others' sakes,)—
I'll not say how they then both whispered,
    "Dear!"
  Then melted in each others arms and—aches!—

I'll stop and stuff this into my portmanteau,
And after dinner finish up the canto.

For now I'm hunting food, and hunting *rest.*
    And who could rest and write of early love?
For, as I write, some half-unwelcome guest
    Comes peering o'er the page, mild as a dove,
And yet it stirreth something in my breast
    To painfulest convulsions, which do move
The deepest soul, and lift the lake of tears
Until it overfloods the bank of years.

My own unrest is sad enough regret;
    And yet, sweet Nameless—I can better bear
My flow of tears than that the violet
    Be faded from thine eyes. O dregs of myrrh!
But then I cannot write these things. They set
    My hand a-tremble, and the white page blur.
O sweet, pure, patient love, I feel thy breast
Throb through the years to mine, *unrest! unrest!*

O, I would give my gold, (but have I much?
    And would I be a poet if I had?)
Would give all my ambition, (and of such
    Have I enough to curse me, as 'tis said?)—
Give—but there is no word can touch
    My passion for a rest! Oh, could I tread

Where once I trod, I know I would not be
Where now I am, but be at rest with thee!

    *   *   *   *   *

I promised I would tell you all about
  Poor Pilgrim's love affair with rosy Lilie,
(Or rather *lily* Lilie; but it's out,
  So let it go as written, sound or silly,)—
His love for her was certainly devout.
  He ought to marry her—the rub is, "*will* he ?"
I think he either will not or he will;
But this, of course, remains a mystery still.

The deepness of their love I could not write.
  The warmness of their love would melt a heart.
The sweetness of their love was such delight,
  'Twas not describable by any art.
'Twas warm, o'erpowering, passionate, full by
    night,
  By day, confiding, tender—Not a part
Of all but what was both. Love's power was
    regal.
'Twas fondly intimate—and yet was legal.

So argued *they*, at least, through all the Spring
  And Summer and the Autumn days. But now

The Winter comes and spreads his frosty wing;
  And frost, that stings like fire, is on each plow
Of steely blue; and scintillations fling   '
  From off the moldboards up to stars that throw
Their scintillations from the gleamy sky,
The moldboard of the universe, on high.

Howl on, ye hideous winds! ye swift-winged
      snows,
  That strike and smart like icy hornets' stings,
Beat! beat! and mock ye Nature's dying throes !
  Howl! beat! O desolating, cruel things!
Little ye dream, and less ye care, God knows,
  The ruin ye are working! O for wings
Of mercy, that I might o'erspread the world
And shield it from this tempest heaven-hurled!

Alas! and there's a special work of ruin
  This cold of winter wrought; for 'tis agreed
That balmy climes make better love, and few in
  The cold of winter love so warmly, need
I mention? Snow-storms block the bliss o'wooin'.
  For man, or maid is so much like a weed,
Affected deeply by the state of weather—
And Love's no stabler than a floating feather.

To make it short, as sad as it may be,
  The fountain of poor Pilgrim's love froze over,

Or *seemed* to freeze, more true; and so, you see,
  He was so fearful and so changed a lover
He broke her heart by coolness; and, for she
  Had given *all* to him.   O God above her!
How could he ravish all she had to prize,
And then, poor girl, neglect her, while she dies?

Man never loves with half the love of woman.
  His purest love is more than half but passion.
The chastest love of the most pure and true man
  Is not so passionless, in any fashion,
As woman's worst.   It surely is not human
  That lusty men should come and lay their
    trash on
The shrine of woman's love, then steal her trust
And flee and leave her but the scars of lust.

'Tis strange how balmy winds may bend young
    trees;
  Stranger how kind young lovers' kindness
    blows
And bends their action by its loving breeze,
  Till what they plant for joys grow knotted woes!
The Pilgrim gets bewildered, so he flees
  And leaves her—turns her flowery spring to
    snows.

All else she bore, but this is Hell—if *this*
She plunge away from, would she do amiss?

See Lilie yonder, with so many scars
    Of soul, and marks without of inner pain—
So young, and yet, in those few days of wars,
    She suffered twenty years! She cried, in vain,
Out in the woe and waste of air. The stars
    Did quiver at her wail, and yet the plain
Died into nothing in the ears of men—
And so then has she heart to cry again?

She standeth quailing at the midnight shimmer
    That floats far down upon the moaning river.
See what a passionate convulsive tremor
    Creeps o'er her frame! She starts! a death-
        cold shiver
Of woes chills her pale as the still moon's glim-
        mer!
    She looks back quick—she leaps—is still for-
        ever!
Blame not. Who knows, O woe - bewildered
    daughter!
Thy secret, save God and the tongueless water.

Men talk about committing suicide,
    But only he, who stands and looks aghast

Into the world beyond, and yet does hide
   Determination then to quit the past—
Leap into the unknown, Hell-deep, dark tide,
   Knows what he talks about ; yet he's the last
To mention of his purpose; so men mock
At him, then fall upon the self-same rock.
'Twere well to think more deeply ere we talk.

   'Twere well to scan the heights of mercy first.
For could we see o'erhead the swooping hawk
   We would not blame the timid quail that durst
Dart swiftly and so headlong 'gainst a rock,
   And thus meet death, rather than face the worst—
And so familiar Death appears less dread
To some sad ones than swooping woe o'erhead.

But why are men fore'er and everlasting
   On suiciding making such a fuss ?
For every single human found a-casting
   Himself from woe to death (poor wretched
      cuss !)
A *thousand* thoughtless people more are blasting
   The vigor of their lives, killed by the muss
And rash excess of *false*, polluting pleasure—
Do they not suicide in the same measure?

Great Jove! I look into the glass, and see
   My eyes stand outward, in a perfect stare,

And pop half from their sockets!   I must flee
   This subject, or, ere I am half aware,
I'll find my own throat cut—so let it be!
   I'd care but little, if I only dare (?)—
Eheu! my very skin crawls with affright,
To think of what I've dared to write to-night!

   .   .   .   .

Ring ! ring ! ring !   O, horror-tongued bell !
   Fall on our ears turned into woeful words!
Ye people, winding in a speechless spell,
   But thinking thoughts more bitter than the
      Lord's,
Ye would consign *her* to the deep of Hell,
   Who sleeps before you, innocent as the birds
That break the sad uncharitable still
By sinless songs of love from every bill.

Cold Pharisaic man, who would forbid
   Her purer erring soul a place with ye,
You would have done the same that Lilie did !
   Young mother, buoyant at the boundless glee
Thy first born showeth, even despite the chide
   Its sterner father gives, how would it be
Were it conceived and born without a name?
Sweet woman, wouldst thou not have done the
      same ?

Warm-hearted man, that *only* would condemn
  Because your moral standard calls it wrong ;
Had you been she, you would have done the same!
  ᛫And maidens, gathering in a weeping throng
Around the wayward dead, ye mourn ᛫the shame
  Of whom, a year ago, ye envied strong—
Ye would have done the same as she, and are,
God knows, her most forgiving mourners far!

I know, too faithful woman—I confess
  That, if my very goodness—all the best
Of all God gave, with which the world to bless,
  Had led *me* where thy love abounding breast
Led *thee*, I should not deem I did amiss
  To shun the train of curses, for the rest
Beyond the River—I would calmly leap
Into the flood and o'er me let it sweep!

Curse on! curse deep! curse well ! ye damned
      tongues,
  Your curses cannot reach beyond the grave.
Damn! damn the innocent, forget her wrongs!
  Thank Heaven ! she does not hear your pious
      rave!
God will restore her what to her belongs.
  The times may come when you will vainly
      crave

What blessings God gives her. She bore the
    worst
Here, *there* ye cursers may become the cursed !

Well, well, there is no need of one man's bat-
    tling
The creeds of all the world of orthodoxies—
It were as useless as the idle prattling
Of busy babes; for Satan has his proxies
E'en 'mong the moral—aye, how many a fatling
    Of Hell is clothed as priest — how many
       hawks' eyes
Look out of doves' meek feathers! Yet—ah ! yet
High Heaven knows them every one, I bet !

Sweet Lilie, O! how art thou bruised and crushed!
    Yet men would stamp thee more—well, let
       them stamp,
The wreck may be transplanted (when all's hushed
    O'er thee), where human feet dare never tramp,
And there leave into life forever flushed
    With love and peace immortal, when every
       scamp
That cursed thee here may wail for "water!
    water!"
And not find it, as thou didst, injured daughter.

And do not too uncharitably judge
  Pilgrim in this calamitous affair.
Fair maids, spare all unnecessary grudge
  Against unfaithful him.   Pull not the hair
Upon a head already sore—fie, fudge!
  He is no worse than many more, who bear
A better public name, whom you let simper
" I love you, dear!" at which you sigh and whim-
      per.

Think you that, when he first was photographed
  In her soul-curtained eyes, he dared to dream
Of anything unkind ?   And when they laughed
  At older warnings, while their faces beam
With fresh young love; and when they over-
      quaffed
  Love, till their hearts, impassioned, Oh! did
      seem
To reel with very drunkenness, until
It stole their prudence and their sterner will;

And they went staggering down a bank of bliss
  And flowering beauty, till they fell, aghast,
Low in the muddy stream and foul abyss
  That bound such banks below at last—
Think you he deemed their chaste and youthful
      kiss,

They then exchanged, would ever be to blast
Her beauteous life? or dreamed where they were
    going,
Swift as the wind, because of their warm wooing?

O what a world of contradictions this!
The very motives, that would prompt a man
To shower on others well-meant gifts of bliss,
    Spread ruin on the very road o'er-run.
A cruel blow seems kinder than a kiss.
. Start to perform the very best you can,
Your kindness seems, at last, to simply end
In tragedy. Be kind, and you offend.

And every pleasant thing that God has given
    Seems but a snare to tangle one in woe;
And every woe, by which a man is driven,
    Drives him where only fruits of blisses grow;
Make life a hell, and that will win you heaven.—
    And he that tastes of happiness below
May break his fiddle for the time to come—
Make your oration *here*, but *there* you must be
    dumb.

God placed in man the golden gift of love,
    And which would be attended with the sweetest
5

Enjoyment with which all of earth could move
  A human heart, although 'tis called the fleetest.
Of *false* love this is true—O land above!
  It surely, heaven, is not thou that meetest
Such love to mortals simply to enhance
The lassitude that followeth the dance!

O for a love that would be warm eternal!
  Unbroken by the coolness of a blast
And unembittered by that thing infernal,
  Propriety, worst foe thou, loving, hast!
Love that is free indeed would be supernal—
  Aye, world! here lies the mystery at last;
That all the *blessings* heaven has bestowed
Are *curses* turned by customs of the crowd!

O, there is bliss indeed in being wed;
  But 'tis not in the wedding of the hand,
Nor in the law of weddings, which is read,
  Nor in the wedding custom does demand.
The bliss of half the wedded ones is dead,
  Because they are not wedded with the band
That never galls—the wed, whose touch and kiss,
At fifty years of age is young with bliss.

The many curses that some preachers claim
  Do follow pleasure, as a punishment

Sent down from God, are not at all His blame.
  They are alone the curses that are sent
On hearts of innocence, (here is the shame!)
  By godless customs! 'Would the veil were rent
From off the truth, till day devour the night,
And pleasure would be, what it should be, *right!*

I do not find the stiffened jackets in
  The works of Christ. They are the devils'
    work,
Who wish to turn all goodness into sin
  And make the gloom of sin—its soulless irk—
Appear as goodness; hence befooled men,
  Beneath their stiffened jackets, bear a dirk
Sheathed in their dismal, devil-given creeds,
Which, when they speak, stabs truth until it bleeds.

'Tis not because of Jesus' sweet Christianity;
  But 'tis because men will pervert the truth,
And twist high Heaven's sane into insanity,
  And cramp our Saviour's mercy into ruth,
And *would* press all the human from humanity,
  And sprinkle whiteness on the heads of youth.
O Jesus! will it ever, ever be
That men can see the mercy thou canst see?

I know a life, the sweetest sacrifice,
  But one, earth ever knew. O, she was great—

Great by the standard of most human eyes,
  And greater in the eyes round Heaven's gate.
Ideal beauty blushed, fell on its knees,
  And stammered, as it tried to emulate
Her beauty; for it did surpass th' ideal—
Her meek unbounded beauty, yet was real.

And she was born a child of rarest song
  And thoughts of mild, yet big, magnificence——
A poetess even when she lay along
  The blooming stream of childhood; and the
    sense
Was riveted to hear her chastened tongue
  Pour forth her written sonnet-eloquence,
In her most song-engifted utterance—
The very blossoms listened in a trance!

So even her beauty, most divinely gifted,
  Stood pouting, envious of her gift of mind.
But, O, her boundless soul seemed ever lifted
  Beyond the reach of selfishness—too kind
To have seen a fly adrift, and not have drifted
  In sympathy, most superfine-refined,
Down with the drowning mote, to reach and weep
Till she could lift the small waif from the deep.

She grew to womanhood.   Financial crash
  Had left her aged father penniless,

And many children, too, to bear the lash
    Of penury; and ease withdrew caress
They once had known, with all its happy flash.
    She was the youngest in their homelessness—
The tenderest of all, yet the divine
Within her would not darken, but would shine.

She snatched the circumstances by the bit
    And charioted her people from despair.
She gave up good renown, that used to flit
    So beauty-sanctified before her, where
She roamed in fields of poesy and wit.
    She smiled above the under-flowing tear,
And turned from beauty, poetry and fame,
To lowly work, a sacrifice for them.

A fast she laid upon her soul! O what
    A graveyard of the grandest hopes she built,
To work for them! What golden wishes she
        forgot,
    To live for them! What monuments, a-gilt
With love, she left half made and left to rot,
    To suffer on for them! What flowers did wi't
That she had digged to plant beside her door
Of life—digged, but unplanted evermore!

And *then*, *because* the world did sympathize
    With her and love, what none could help but
        love,
And marvel at her willing sacrifice,
    They *envied* her the little praise, and wove
A subtle net of ruinous treacheries:
    And still she found no fault, and did not move
From out her path of kindness; but she wept
Her grief alone, while those who cursed her slept.

She bore it silently, tho' painfully,
    Until it froze the roses on her cheek,
And slew the smile that wantoned in her eye—
    Still she remembered " Blessed are the meek!"
At last they stigmatized the purity
    Of one too pure for earth ; and then, to break
The last chord in her heart, forgiving, kind,
They drove from home, the injured pure in mind!

And yet their spite went after her afar,
    Until the poison from their serpent hiss
Stung deeper in the daily opened scar—
    Rebroke her broken heart ! And this, ah, this
Was more than such a woman's heart could bear,
    And so—she died ! Then Jesus stooped to
        kiss

And dress the wounds with leaves of Gilead ;
For *there* was balm, which turned the sad to glad !

Well, so it is: the ones who give their all
   Unselfishly to others, get least thanks below;
And hence it is I wonder, and I call
   This life a contradiction.   It is so.
The selfish get the sweets, the kind the gall—
   The cruel get the weal, the kind the woe.
The world's too mean to learn the reason why;
And so the best and kindest quickest die.

   .   .   .   .

We know but little of poor Pilgrim's pains,
   He nursed, then loathed, then blessed, then
      cursed, by turns.
The soul forever after knowledge strains,
   Although 'tis *sorrow* to the heart that *learns*—
And yet the heart of man wails out complains,
   If life refuses more of " sorrow"—yearns
For more of " knowledge ! knowledge !" tho' it
      knows
'Tis always pickled in the juice of woes!

I know but little of poor Pilgrim's pain;
   But this I know, 'twas surely deep of soul.

'Twas much as he could do to bear the strain
   That broke the strings of her sweet lyre with
      dole.
God pity what kept dancing in his brain!
   Sometimes he almost lost his self-control.
Sometimes he trembled with a half-begot
Desire to go where Lilie was—widl thought !

Had men been more forgiving to those two,
   And not bewildered them with their damnation,
Of course, they would have wed and journeyed
      thro'
   A useful life together.—Desolation,
Despair and Death had lost, at least, a few
   Morsels to glut their greedy desperation.
Both erred at first ; *he* sinned at last ; but men
Are half responsible for Pilgrim's sin.

Well, well, altho' each has a life within
   That may be sad forever, yet one must
Pursue an outward course, amid earth's din,
   That is not always so bowed in the dust.
Outside a medley picture hangs to win—
   One must not be big fool enough to trust
His inner life to lie in public gaze,
But smile and act lies in a thousand ways.

So, Pilgrim, we will drop this horrid matter,
  And send you on your falsifying way.
Remember this tho': "Don't go near the water!"
  Remember, too, your tragical affray,
When you would woo again a frail fair daughter.
  Now lift your hat and bid the past "good day!"
And go—the Lord knows where, and so do I,
And I will tell the public "by and by."

What histories are writ in "by and by!"
  The buxom country lass laughs out, at eve,
"Ha! Jake will be here, by and by, and I—
  Won't I be jolly then, you better b'lieve!
And kiss him, with a, 'how is that for high?'"
  Ah! how her happy healthy spirits heave!
But then—Jake doesn't come, alas! and so
It grows into a "by and by" of woe!

Our joys are half made up of "by-and-bys,"
  Which we expect here to participate,
How few of which we ever realize!
  We are not now, but "by and by" are, great.
We now are blind, but "by and by" have eyes.
  But one thing certain, if we only wait
And work in godly patience, you and I
Will grasp the whole in yon great "By-and-by."

O Ellen, with your holy violet eye!
  O thousand promises of " by-and-by!"
O expectation born to smile and die!
  O " by-and-by," thou unintended lie!
O may we not yet realize, on high,
  The promises and all the memory
Of what we *hoped* to have beneath the sky,
At least, above it in *the* " by-and-by ?"

Now " comes the tug of war " in truth; for now
  There are the howls, the roar, the crack, the
    crash,
The yells, the oaths, the wails, the rush, the row,
  The screams, the cries, the shouts, the fire, the
    flash,
The tears, the blood, the thud, the wounds, the
  woe,
  The cuts, the breaks, the prayers, the deaths,
    the gash,
The curse, the damn, the hopes, the fears, the
  scars,
The smoke—aye, *all* the hideousness of wars!

And yet men preach and preach for more recruits
  To gorge this hideousness, with all the zeal
Christ's ministers would show for Him. The
    brutes

Stand still, pop-eyed, to see us humans reel,
Dead-drunk with blood. What horrid blastful
    fruits
Grow on the tree of war! Men make a meal
Of other men, thus fat themselves for others
Again to fat on—this is war, my brothers!

Well, Pilgrim he was fool enough, (or wise
    Enough, or what you please,) to go to war.
I'll tell you how it happened, to tell no lies:
    He still was bleeding from the open scar
Of most disastrous love. O how he tries
    To sew it up! but tries it vainly; for
The stitches rip; and so—ah! sad mishap!
At every stitch more ghastly grows the gap!

It isn't many steps down from the blues
    Unto despair, and he for sure had got them.
The way I generally have them "beats the Jews;"
    But now, just now, I'm free of them, let rot
      them!
He looked at Uncle Sam's big "gun-boat" shoes
    And thought them better than he once had
      thought them.
He thought he surely could not make it worse;
Besides an *office* might refill his purse!

He thought of living, then he thought of dying,
 Then thought he cared but little which he did,
He thought of what had past, then fell to crying;
 He thought of bullets, then he sat and slid
Down on a plank of glory—sat defying
 His fears—then roused and tried to rid
Himself of that most hateful thought, the curse
Of going to his grave without a hearse.

Well, after he had sat, and sat, and brooded
 Upon this subject till he thought he knew
The whole of it, I think he had concluded
 To stay at home—just then an old cock crew!
And then his resolution he denuded
 Of all its gloss, and saw that it was true,
He had denied his country; so the man
Ran o'er the whole thing in his mind again.

And, when he came around again, of course,
 He ended with the self-same resolution,
" I do deny my country!"   Loud and hoarse
 The old cock crew again.   Confusion
Took hold of Pilgrim; but he had to force
 His thought o'er it again; but some delusion
Made him deny again; and, growing wroth,
He said : " I will deny thee, country! " with an
      oath.

And then the old cock crew so sad, so loud—
  He burst his mighty heart, and fell and died !
Then Pilgrim went and wound him in a shroud—
  Bore him to the potato-patch, and cried,
And laid him in the ground ; the while a crowd
  Of wondering, weeping hens, with heads askew,
     soft sighed
To hear clods fall on chiefest of the cocks,
And asked each other, " was he orthodox ? "

That made him think of how *he* might grow fa-
     mous,
  By crowing others into ranks ; and so
He turned recruiting officer—to shame us!
  He thought, " Oh, if I die from overflow
Of patriotism, surely that a glorious name is—
  Die by o'ercrowing, like the cock, you know.
Oh ! how the patriotic maids will stand and weep
Above me, strewing flowers where I sleep !"

And so he went to shouting, *shouting*, SHOUTING,
  " RECRUITS !" and finally became a colonel.
Ah ! any one could go to war, *sans* pouting
  For so much fame—and pay!   O, this eternal
Blab over military glory, I feel like scouting !
  The men that get the name be most infernal

Cowards, as a rule, and hide behind, and grumble
At, those who earn the crown for them—the
        humble!

I did it once, that is, I stood afront
    These famous cowards, to help to win their
        crown
Of glittering glory—bore the blasted brunt
    Of hardship for the few—for their renown.
I lived a life in death for them. I wont
    Be fool enough to do't again: I've grown
More sparing of my flesh and bone since then—
Grown older—selfisher—like other men.

Well, Pilgrim went to war; and he, they say,
    Was quite the youngest and the handsomest
Commissioned colonel in the " late affray."
    O, what conflicting thoughts warred in his
        breast !
He tried to throw his memories away,
    And think of fame; he dare not think of rest,
It always had the opposite effect,
Unrest, because it made him recollect.

But Pilgrim went to war—but did not go
    Because he loved his country (though he did),
But went to one war just to shun the woe

Of other war (within), and there was need
Of some such move, from what I know
   And what you know, for I've told you—forbid
Not Pilgrim this escape, or he might rave
Himself too early to a humble grave !

So Pilgrim went to war, and so did many;
   But out of all the thousands men that went,
Less went for country than went for the penny—
That is the pay.   But, of these few God sent
For patriots, one was my brother Bennie.
   For country and for God Ben pitched his tent—
But then you're unacquainted with my brother,
And so I must explain, confound the bother!

His face was thinner than a common razor;
   His hair was blacker than a common crow's;
He tried a mustache, but he could'nt "raise her;"
   He limped from corns and bunions on his toes;
And, when he passed a lady, he would sure amaze
     her
   By blushing, whereupon he'd blow his nose
"To put it off" (to use a common term)
Then whistle off the danger of her charm.

Just five feet in his boots, and not much taller
   When out of them—with little, meek black
     eyes !

His neck so short he scarce could wear a collar.
　　But Ben was nimble as the nimblest flies,
And flies were quick as Ben, and not much
　　　　smaller.
　　He never sees a woman but he shies,
And yet he loves them all—and all men too;
And so he loves his country, loves his God, and
　　　　you !

A pillar in the church ! and, though so small
　　A pillar, still he held a greater weight
Than any other pillar of them all.
　　Of all words in his dictionary "hate"
He thought the strangest word.　He would not
　　　call . . .
　　But, Ben, no matter if you are so great,
I've many other things to talk about,
So I can't stop for you—I drop you out!

So Pilgrim went to war—and so did I.
　　He went to war because he was a colonel;
I went because—because I knew not why.
　　The whole thing, anyhow, was most infernal;
And all will come to see it by and by.
　　But, if infernal, or supernal, or eternal
Disgrace or honor, let it be; but, anyhow,
I hope it is the last such horrid row.

Well, Pilgrim went to war.   God bless the cock
  That crew him into it!   It did him good,
If not the "cause."   He fell upon the rock,
  By that manœuver, otherwise it would
Have fall'n on him.   He led the passive flock
  Of twice five hundred men, and—ate his food.
To make it short, here, let me, reader, say,
His regiment chanced on a fight one day.

They fought right well; so much so, I suppose,
  That Pilgrim thought it quite unnecessary
For him to help; and so I saw his nose,
  (Oh! beautiful! I tell you he was wary!)
Stuck from behind a tree.   His voice arose—
  Crew loud and long and patriotic very—
But let me add here, what's more to his credit,
That, though that once, he never after did it.

So Pilgrim went to war, and served—one hundred
    days;
  And so he grew not very battle-gory.
He fought one battle (only), and his ways
  Were strange in that—at least, so goes the story.
He shouts commands, his regiment obeys—
  Their own desires; he gets the glory,
The hero colonel, who embraced the tree,
The handsome colonel aged twenty three.

  6

Wild ran his thoughts the day he left the army,
  Or rather jumped by fits and starts and stops.
Remorse turns sometimes stillest lives most stormy.

  .   .   .   .   .   .

  He sleeps.   Dear sleep ! here troubles curtain
      drops.
Life has no other gift so pleasant for me.
  Some think they find in juices of the hops
A pleasanter.   Well, let him sleep, poor fellow,
Perhaps his sorrows, while he sleeps, may mellow.

  .   .   .   .   .   .

  .   .   .   .   .   .

Go to, and tattle! yea, go to, and babble!
  Tell all the truth and five times more of lies!
Nor stop to think, that but the low-bred rabble
  Would stoop to taint their tongues; for never
      pries
A cultured man, but fools and asses dabble
  In what is none their business. All the "whys?"
And " wherefores ?' of all people's business, but
  .   their own,
Lie with the lower-bred—with them alone.

Besides the greater curse of tattling is,
  'Tis always 'gainst the better, worthier ones.
The really bad and low are free from this,

The ones that fill the social, moral thrones,
Are slandered. Serpents do not care to hiss
  At foul low toads, but shake their rattle-bones
And spit at higher beings in the scale,
At humans. O thou cursed "tattle-tale !"

The wind is up to-night, my spirits down;
  And sadness sits with low and bowèd head
Beneath the shadow of my misnamed frown;
  ("For when were sad, oft people call us mad.")
I'm sad; for slander sneaketh thro' the town—
  A damning shadow moving an a tread.
'Tis touching some one's head snow-white with
      grief;
And yet the pitiless crowd give their belief!

I know she must be innocent, by how
  The tale is told; none tells a fact; each gives
An unformed surmise—then they haste to throw
  A curse at her. I trace it back : the sieves
Catch less and less at every sifting, so
  It comes to nothing—yet it grows and lives—
Ah! yonder now the pretty victim goes;
O beautiful! and purer than the snows!

Aye, there's the rub, if it were otherwise
  She would not then be slandered! See her lip

A-quiver with the pain! Her lustrous eyes
　　Grown dull by soaking in the tears that drip
Night unto night! How people mock her sighs!
　　How heavy lift the feet that used to trip
Light as the day! God, love her in her sadness!
Her sorrow is the fiendish tattler's gladness.

Some time ago we left the colonel sleeping;
　　(For men now took to calling Pilgrim colonel.)
And thus it is that those who do least reaping
　　Get most the spoils of wars. The privates *earn*
　　　all,
The leaders get all, to make the assertion sweeping,
　　And so get rid a subject so infernal!
I said we left the colonel sleeping, and
That's true, we did, I'd have you understand.

His sleep however did not seem to rest him.
　　He traveled forty thousand miles in thought.
I think he'll tell his dream, if you request him.
　　I only know this much, and that I got
From the convulsive jerks that did molest him
　　And snatches from his speech—the plot
Of *all* his dream was too clandestine deep
For me to read the whole he thought asleep.

He went almost two times around the world;
　　·And, every step he took, he stumbled over

Old memories in his fall; and there was swirled
  A sea of blood about him; and would hover
Old footsteps back of him; and, when he whirled,
    The ghost of one once beautiful reached for
      the rover;
And then this vision would be broken by
A fall o'er an open grave, where, lying nigh,

Another hope breathed out its last; and then
  He grasped his eyes, as from his memory
A flash, like lightning o'er a battle plain,
  Streamed out and glimmered far and nigh
About him o'er the blood and corpses, slain,
  Of hopes—O God! of *everything* could die
And he could wish to live!—and then it darkened;
And so he stumbled on, and shook and hearkened.

It flashed again, and he stood up afront
  A leaning tombstone, where gleamed in the
    light
A name red-writ by blood and by the brunt
  Pen of despair—name, *Lilie!* he reeled to
    right—
A thousand slanderous fingers seemed to point
  Out of the dimmer dark.   He cursed the bit-
    ter sight,

And shut his eyes and stumbled on; till, lo!
He stumbled in a river red with woe!

He heard the splash and heard the hideous scream
   Of a drowning woman, interluded by
Her prayers for him, who sent her there. The
     stream
   Reached up. She uttered one wild cry—
It broke the quietude, and—broke his dream! ·
   He started out of sleep! His lips were dry!
His face was white! His hands did tremble; and
His heart seemed bursting from its mortal band!

One poet sings, " life is an empty dream!"
   Another sings the opposite, and says
'Tis real and is earnest!" Well, we deem
   That both are right and both are wrong (strange
     phrase)—
As if the things we see in dreaming only seem !
   Aye, they are real earnest, and do craze
Some minds. Life is a sort of dream, I know—
A real dream, and earnest with its woe!

Some people's lives are one long night-mare sleep
   Of misery. They try to shriek—to cry
Themselves awake, but cannot—O, how deep
   Their slumber! and how desolate they lie, ·

And cannot stir a toe, or even weep!
O, they would give a world to wake, or die!
Ah! you, who know the dread of night-mare, go
Pity those stretched in the night-mare of their woe!

Some revel in a perfect bliss, I know—
A dream, in youth's luxuriant love, of sweets
They think to wake to after they shall grow
Some older. The morning of their manhood
beats
The gong for breakfast at their heads; and, lo!
They wake but to partake of chaffs and cheats,
And turn and curse the bed of roses and of bliss
They pillowed on, and sigh, "Ah, well, I wis!"

Some lives dream on and on, but dream no thing
Of much importance—dream of platitude,
And talk their dreams aloud. Some sing
A dream of beauties destitute of good.
Some dream, and, as they dream, they swing
Sometimes beyond this worldly amplitude
And bring back, from the region of a star,
Some thing, some thought—grand, glorious, from
afar!

These are the geniuses, sublime of head.
Some dream forever out beyond the crowd

And whisper them to us; these are the dead.
  Some dream forever, altho' never loud,
Low down by buried coffins they have wed.
  Some sleep, and, dumber than one in a shroud,
Dream nothing; these are what I call the " sticks!"
Some dream but dissipations; these are " bricks!"

.

BE IT SO.

WHAT framer of imaginations
has not his platitudes ?
And mine is on me.
Light and dull as withered cornstalks.
My brain lies in its sheathing,
Like juiceless pumice in a cider press.
I laugh at nothings—
Stare blank at keenest of wit-faces.
My fancies glut themselves on nothings,
Satisfied.
The sun-engilded cloud,
That swings along the sunset, like a censer,
Is nothing more magnificent to-day
Than tumble-weeds
Rolling over the sered Winter-fields.
The green leaves, the tracts of the Church of
      Nature,
Shaking at us eloquent, betimes,
To-day are utter blank tracts—
Poor brown paper—unwritten, unattractive.

The bird-songs,
On which my fond•imaginings have sailed,
In infinite speed, in infinite beauty, in infinite
      purity,
Up to the gates of a new born Eden,
To-day sound as the clamorous croak of frogs.
The glimmering river,
On which have floated I, entranced in vision,
Out to the LIMITLESS, and said:
"The river of God's peace falling into infinity—
Grand sublimity!"
To-day 'tis as the murky play-puddle of the street-
      boys.
Over me the blue skies hangs as a faded dim-blue
      awning,
Undelightful.
The beauty of a woman's eye is as a broken gog-
      gle-glass,
Lying in the dusty street, dull-gleaming,
Uncoveted.
The redness of a woman's cheek for loveliness,
Is as the red bricks 'neath my feet.
The voluptuousness of her bosom
And deepness of the passions of her rounded
      beauties
Are flat commonness—

Unenticing as the rattling skeleton in my study.
My aspirations, dropt from the ceiling of my mind,
Like crumbling plaster,
Are swept out unregretted.
My hopes are bees in Winter,
Blank—aimless!
One lone hill of thought thrust up on this level,
Repeated at long intervals.
This the little flowerless thought-hill:
" What is man, that thou art mindful of him?"
Verily! verily!

.

What shall I write then? What
Shall be the goal, the finish of the thought?
I've followed on the trail, till that I sought
Is seen a gauzy glimmering ; and I know not
If it be some immortal ending of a thought
Far in the Heaven, or flash of nothing near—
A firefly near, or window light beyond it thro'
The tossing trees, or rising star set in the blue!
But I see no more of it—a tear
Has put it out! What shall I write then? What

Shall be the finish of the feeling wrought?
I write—I look—I see . . . a blotted spot!
So what I yearn to write is written . . . not;
And what is written here, compared to what
I would were writ, is as a blot !

www.ingramcontent.com/pod-product-compliance
Lightning Source LLC
Chambersburg PA
CBHW032251080426
42735CB00008B/1089